T0162441

Self-Knowledge

This title is now available as
an eBook and audiobook.

Self-Knowledge

The School of Life

Published in 2017 by The School of Life
First published in the USA in 2018
930 High Road, London, N12 9RT
Copyright © The School of Life 2017
Designed and typeset by Marcia Mihotich
Printed in Latvia by Livonia Print

A proportion of this book has appeared online at
www.theschooloflife.com/thebookoflife

The School of Life is a resource for helping us understand
ourselves, for improving our relationships, our careers and our
social lives – as well as for helping us find calm and get more
out of our leisure hours. We do this through creating films,
workshops, books, apps and gifts.

www.theschooloflife.com

ISBN 978-0-9957535-0-1

10 9

Contents

I
Self-Ignorance

One of the most striking features of our minds is how little we understand them. Although we inhabit ourselves, we seldom manage to make sense of more than a fraction of who we are. It can be easier to master the dynamics of another planet than to grasp what is at play in the folds of our own brains.

Instances of self-ignorance regularly surprise and perturb us: on certain days, we can be irritable or sad without any idea why. Or we may feel lost in our career, but be unable to say more than that we wish to 'do something creative' or 'help to make the world a better place' – plans so vague that they leave us vulnerable to the more robust plans of others.

It has been the achievement of psychology to instil in us a sense of a basic division between two parts of the mind: the conscious and the unconscious; between what is immediately accessible to us and what lies in shadow, and will surprise us in symptoms, dreams, slips of the tongue and diffuse anxieties, longings and fears. It has also been the work of psychology to insist that maturity must involve a constant drive to turn what is unconscious conscious; to help us master the art of self-knowledge.

It can be easier to master the dynamics of another planet than to grasp what is at play in the folds of our own brains.

We need not blame ourselves for our poor grasp of our own minds. The problem is inherent in the very architecture of the brain, an organ that evolved over millennia for the sake of rapid, instinctive decision-making – not the patient, introspective sifting of ideas and emotions.

However, a degree of emotional squeamishness is also responsible for our failure to look inside. A lot of what is unconscious is tricky material that we shy away from looking at too closely. For example, we may feel troublingly angry towards people we thought we loved. We may be more ruthless and envious than nice people are ever meant to be. We may have to make enormous changes to our lives, but prefer the ease of the status quo. Across childhood, we may have had instilled in us, so subtly we didn't even notice, strong notions about what are normal and not normal things to experience. Traditionally, boys were not allowed to acknowledge that they felt like crying, and girls weren't allowed to entertain certain kinds of ambitions for fear of being unladylike.

We might not have such obviously naive prohibitions today, but other, equally powerful, ones may have taken their place. We may have picked up covert but forceful indications that no decent person (no-one loved by their parents, at least) could be unable to cope at work, be tempted by an affair, or still be upset over a break-up that took place three years ago. Most of our sexual desires still have no place in our standard understanding of respectability.

When difficult feelings threaten to emerge, the light of consciousness can be counted upon to take fright and shine its beam elsewhere. By failing to investigate the recesses of the mind, we carefully protect our self-image and can continue to think well of ourselves. However, we don't escape from the job of introspection lightly. There is almost always a high price to pay for our reluctance to look within. Feelings and desires that have not been examined tend not to leave us alone; they linger and spread their energy randomly to neighbouring issues. Ambition that doesn't know itself comes out as anxiety. Envy comes out as bitterness; anger turns into rage; sadness evolves into depression. Disavowed material buckles and strains the system. We develop pernicious tics; a facial twitch, impotence, an incapacity to work, alcoholism, a porn compulsion. Most so-called 'addictions' are at heart symptoms of insistent difficult feelings that we haven't found a way to address. Insomnia is revenge for thoughts we have refused to have in the day.

Strangers to ourselves, we end up making bad choices: we exit a relationship that might have been quite workable. We don't explore our own professional talents in time. We alienate friends through erratic, off-putting behaviour. We lack insight into how we come across to others and appal or shock them. We buy the wrong things and go on holiday to places that have little to do with what we really enjoy.

It is no coincidence that Socrates should have boiled down the entire wisdom of philosophy to one simple command: *Know Yourself*. This is a distinctly odd-sounding ambition. Society has no shortage of people and organisations offering to guide us around distant continents, but very few that will help us with the arguably far more important task of travelling around the byways of our own minds. Fortunately, however, there are a number of tools and practices that can help us to reach inside our minds and move us from dangerous vagueness to challenging but redeeming clarity.

II
Philosophical
Meditation

Insofar as society encourages us to spend time in our minds, it allots particular prestige to a set of practices collectively referred to by the term 'meditation'. Adherents of meditation typically recommend that we sit in a particular position and strive to empty our consciousness of its normal medley of feelings and ideas. We should still the agitations of what the Buddhists have evocatively termed our 'monkey minds' in a bid for serenity.

There is another approach to consider, not based on Eastern thought, but on ideas that have come down to us from the Western philosophical tradition. We term it Philosophical Meditation, a practice with the premise that a decisive share of the trouble in our minds comes from thoughts and feelings that have not been untangled, examined and confronted with sufficient attention.

Philosophical Meditation needs a time of the day when nothing much will be expected of us. We might be in bed or on the sofa, alone with a notepad and pen. Key to the practice are three well-angled questions:

— *What am I presently anxious about?*
— *What am I presently upset about?*
— *What am I presently excited about?*

Anxiety

We start the Philosophical Meditation by asking: What am I presently anxious about?

Life is generally far more alarming than we allow ourselves to accept. We constantly have to navigate an uncertain world. We are permanent hostages to the whims of fortune. Every minute of the waking day, a skittish radar in one part of our minds is scanning the vast, partly misty, horizon and noting new sources of uncertainty and risk: what will the meeting be like? When do we need to leave? What happened with the letters? Where are we going to be five years from now? Where is the nearest bathroom? We are never more than one piece of bad luck away from a stroke, disgrace or ruin.

During our meditative session, we need to give all our anxieties a chance to understand themselves, for three-quarters of our agitation is not that there are things to worry about, but that we haven't given our worries the time they require to be understood and defused. Only by being listened to can anxieties be drained of some of their intensity. If we were to record our own stream of consciousness in moods of agitation, the result would tumble out in chaotic confusion: '... the biscuits thing all over again, why, why, why, idiot, God the Seoul deal, they can't do it, I have to do it, the bathroom now, I can't do it at 10.30 tomorrow with Luke, why get myself into this, the stupid invoice, why me, my fault, the tree branches, couldn't sleep ...'

This fast-moving stream can be gradually tamed, drained, driven into rivulets and evaporated into something far less daunting. Our overall nervousness declines when our anxieties are systematically laid out and examined.

We need to grip our anxieties head on and force ourselves to imagine what might happen if their vague catastrophic forebodings truly came to pass: what would happen to us if everything we are dimly worried about really came to pass? What are the real dangers? How might we still be OK, even if it all fell apart? Entertaining the most extreme consequences can be the best way to finally neuter an otherwise nagging concern. One by one, we should confront the worst, and see that it is, for the most part, very survivable.

Exercise:
Interpreting
Anxiety

Write down what you are anxious about; find at least eight things. Each entry should only be a single word (or just a few words) at this point. Don't worry if some of the anxieties look either incredibly trivial or tragi-comically large. If you're having trouble, search for things that may be anxiety-inducing under the following categories:

- *Work*
- *Relationships*
- *Children/Parents*
- *Health*
- *Money*
- *Things I have to do*

Feel the curious release that can come from just making a list of these items.

Huge relief can now come from what we call 'unpacking' an anxiety. There are two kinds of unpacking we might do around any given anxiety.

1. Practical unpacking

Walk yourself through the practical challenge. Ask the following questions:

- *What steps do you need to take?*
- *What do others need to do?*
- *What needs to happen when?*

It is very useful to have a calm and sympathetic part of yourself (or a friend) listening in on the detailed description of what needs to be done to address an issue. It is no longer merely an anxiety; it is a set of steps. They might not all be easy, but at least you are clearer about what they are.

2. Emotional unpacking

Talk yourself through an emotional challenge or set of doubts. Describe the feeling in more detail. What do you feel it points to? Imagine trying to piece it together for a very considerate friend.

The aim here isn't to solve all anxieties; it's to start to get to know them and to experience the relief that comes from this.

Upset

We are ready to turn to the second guiding enquiry behind the Philosophical Meditation: What am I presently upset about?

This could sound odd, because we may have no particular sense of being upset about anything. But the claim here is that we are almost always likely to be upset about something, for the simple reason that we are far more vulnerable than we think and that life constantly places us in the line of fire of little arrows fired by people around us. Without meaning to, our partners and friends daily shoot small darts at us: they didn't ask how the day went, they have forgotten that we have a meeting, they left the towels in a heap.... It is from such small humiliations and slights that large blocks of resentment eventually form and render us, for example, unable to love or to bear to be touched. Too much of social existence requires an excessive degree of stoicism from us. There are heavy incentives for us not to feel or notice our pains. Eventually, this unacknowledged distress may sink our entire characters into depression.

During our introspective sessions, we can throw off our customary and dangerous bravery and let our sadness take its natural, due shape. There may not be an immediate solution to many of our sorrows, but it helps immeasurably to know their contours. As we turn over our sadnesses, large and small, we might imagine we are discussing them with an extremely kind and patient figure who would give us the chance to evoke the hurt in great detail; someone with whom there would be no pressure to rush, be grown-up or brave and who would allow us to admit without fear to the many things that cause us upset. We should, in introspecting, be maximally indulgent with ourselves as a corrective to our normal tendency to be a bit brutal and to insist that we're getting worked up about nothing – when all along, our pain requires a hearing. In the early 19th century, the German poet Heinrich Heine wrote a poem entitled *Lorelei*, which opens with a candid admission:

Ich weiß nicht, was soll es bedeuten,
Daß ich so traurig bin;

(I don't know what it means
That I'm so sad at heart.)

The premise here is that there are always some very good reasons why we are sad; it's just that we haven't allowed ourselves to feel them, because we labour under unfair assumptions about what it is right and normal to feel sad about.

Exercise:
Interpreting
Upset

As quickly as you can, and without bothering how petty, unreasonable or pretentious it might sound, write a list of current upsets. The more the better. How have others hurt you? What are you sad, nostalgic or wounded about?

Allow yourself in the present safety of this exercise to be, for instance, furious about the way your partner brushes their teeth (too lackadaisical or too smug); the agents of global politics; your boss saying 'yeah, right' in a slightly sarcastic manner; the hotel receptionist who implied you might not be very well off, or your mother commenting on your taste in shoes. These are just starting points and all are valid.

Now ask yourself: If this had happened to a friend, how would you advise them? What might you say?

Again, we're not attempting to resolve these issues as yet. The primary, crucial issue is to be clear about what is actually distressing us. We're allowing our troubles to acknowledge themselves.

Excitement

There is a third question we should consider within a Philosophical Meditation: what am I presently excited about?

Our minds are prone to become clogged up by unexamined sources of excitement that can, once they are decoded, point the way to important changes we might want to make in our lives. An excitement is a curious kind of signpost to new directions we might take, usually in our working or personal lives. We might experience it when we read an article in the newspaper about a new kind of business or hear of a colleague's plans to relocate to another city, but often we don't pause to analyse the excitement any further and thereby miss out on opportunities for development.

All of us have impulses towards growth and development and, when we are alert, can perceive slightly better versions of ourselves thanks to the messages we are receiving in garbled forms via our pulses of interest. The job of introspection is to help us ask ourselves: if this attractive experience (it might be a view, a book, a place, a biography) could talk, what might it want to tell me? Who is it inviting me to be? If other parts of my life were more like this, how might things go? Anything that arouses our curiosity or yields a certain pleasure is providing data – in a slightly illegible form – about something important missing or in short supply in our lives. We should pause to acknowledge the direction we are being inarticulately but perhaps wisely pointed towards.

Exercise:
Interpreting
Excitement

Rapidly list several things that have caught your attention and excited your interest since the last Meditation. A word or a brief phrase is sufficient for now.

Your list might include:

- Moments of envy
- Daydreams: ideas about how life might ideally be
- How nice someone or something was

Pass these through a sieve of further questions:

- Describe your excitement as if to a sympathetic, interested friend.
- If you could realistically change your life in certain ways, what would it be to change in the light of this?
- This exciting thing holds a clue to what is missing in your life; what might that be?
- If this thing could talk, what might it tell you?
- If this thing could try to change your life, what changes might it advise?

Philosophical Meditation does not magically solve problems, but it may help hugely in creating an occasion when we can identify our thoughts and get them in some kind of order. Fears, resentments and hopes become easier to name. We become less scared of the contents of our own minds; we grow calmer, less resentful and clearer about our direction in life. We start, at last, to know ourselves a little better.

III
Emotional
Identity

Our personalities can usefully be divided up into a range of different identities, each of which sheds light on a specific side of who we are: a political identity, a sartorial identity, a financial identity, a culinary identity, and so on.

Perhaps the most important and telling of these identities is our Emotional Identity: the characteristic way in which our desires and fears manifest themselves and our personalities respond to the behaviour – negative and positive – of others. There are four main themes around which our Emotional Identities are structured:

– Self-Love
– Candour
– Communication
– Trust

It is their particular dosage and arrangement within us that decisively shapes who we are.

To get to know ourselves is in large part a question of coming to understanding the distinctive configuration of our Emotional Identity.

Self-Love

Self-love is at the core of answering the riddle of who we are emotionally. It is this quality that determines the extent to which a person feels warmly towards themselves, can forgive and accept who they are, and is able to remain steadfast in the face of opposition and reversals.

Evidence of our degree of self-love emerges particularly clearly around the threats posed to us by other people. When we meet a stranger who has things that we don't (a better job, a nicer partner, etc.), when self-love is low, we may quickly feel ourselves worthless and pitiful. Or, if our levels of self-love are more substantial, we may remain assured by the decency of what we already have and who we are. When another person frustrates or humiliates us, we may be able to let the insult go and even shrug it off, confident in our right to exist, or we may need to enforce respect from others, remaining brooding and devastated, cut to the core of our being by a few unkind words. When we are faced with a need to risk making a fool of ourselves, we may feel the danger to be far too great, or we might be able to withstand the disapproval of others due to a sufficient degree of internal ballast.

The strength and nature of our self-love can be tracked with particular clarity within relationships. When a love affair isn't working for us (perhaps because we're getting hurt or ignored), do we have enough self-love to leave it quickly? Or are we so down on ourselves that we carry an implicit belief that harm is all we deserve from close relationships? In a different vein, when in love, how good are we at apologising for things that may be our fault? If we have sizeable reserves of self-love, we might feel we can afford to admit mistakes and still believe in our basic decency. Yet if our self-love is very fragile, no admission of guilt or error is ever possible; it would sap the last of our limited self-regard. We become very brittle to be around.

In the bedroom, how clean and natural or alternatively disgusting and sinful do our desires feel? If there is a sufficient quantity of self-love in our personalities, it will be possible to recognise that one's desires are – admittedly – sometimes a bit odd, but not feel that they are bad or dark. They can't really be, since we have them and are inwardly sure that we are not inherently sinful. We don't have to be ashamed of ourselves.

Self-love is a factor in our working lives too, determining how much, at the office, we can assert our needs. Do we have a reasonable, well-grounded sense of our worth and so feel able to ask for (and properly expect to get) the conditions that enable us to work most effectively? The issue of self-love decides how independent we can be, how well we can hold onto a thought-through idea that we believe is right when others don't get it. With high enough levels of self-love, we can say no; we are not committed to manic people-pleasing. We may also be able to ask for a raise when we feel we deserve it. We are aware of our genuine contribution. Honourable self-love is not selfishness: it's the feeling of correctly respecting ourselves.

Honourable
self-love is not
selfishness:
it's the feeling
of correctly
respecting
ourselves.

Candour

Candour is another key constituent of our Emotional Identity. The degree to which someone possesses this quality determines the extent to which difficult ideas and troubling facts can be consciously admitted into the mind, soberly explored and taken seriously. How much can we admit to ourselves about who we are – even if, or especially when, it's not very nice? How much do we need to insist on our own normality and sanity? Can we explore our own minds and look into their darker and more troubled corners without flinching too much? Can we admit mistakes? Can we admit to envy, sadness and confusion?

Around others, how ready are we to learn? Do we need always to be defensive, taking a criticism of one part of us as an attack on everything about us? How quickly do we put up a barrier when there is feedback? How ready are we to learn, given that valuable lessons usually come in painful guises?

Communication

Our Emotional Identity is further brought into focus by looking at our communicative styles. Can we put our disappointments into words that, more or less, enable others to see our point? Or do we internalise pain, act it out symbolically or discharge it onto innocents with counterproductive rage?

When other people upset us, do we feel it is OK to communicate our internal state? Do we feel we have the right to let others understand us? Are we sulkers? In other words, when the desired response isn't forthcoming do we quickly give up and go in for aggressive silence? Or can we have a plausible second go: can we take seriously the thought that the other person isn't necessarily evil or stupid? Can we be calm enough to teach? To what degree can we admit that it is legitimate for others not to understand us, and additionally feel that there is a plausible, convincing journey we can take them on towards a proper appreciation of our point of view?

Trust

When it comes to Emotional Identity, trust concerns our instinctive feelings about how safe or dangerous we, other people and the wider world are likely to be. We can have greater or lesser degrees of trust in our capacity to survive challenges. Theoretically we know that a speech, a performance review, a romantic rejection or a bout of financial trouble won't necessarily be life-threatening, but internally they may feel like an enormous danger.

A degree of stress is often called for, but its overall level is very individual. How close are we, at any time, to catastrophe? Around others, how much do we suspect that people are, at heart, out to get us? Are strangers generally nice or likely to be quite nasty? Do we generally imagine new acquaintances will like us or wound us? How fragile are others? If we are a touch assertive, will others collapse and break, or remain more or less fine?

Around love, degrees of trust determine our anxiety about the future with our partner. How tightly do we need to cling to them? If they go off us for a bit, will they return? How much do we imagine we would suffer if they don't come back? How 'controlling' do we need to be? Does such controlling behaviour stem from a basic lack of trust in the other person? How much of a risk can we take? Can we approach an interesting-looking stranger? Can we make the first move around a kiss or sex?

At work, how resilient are we? Failure isn't appealing, but does one see the world as a forgiving place in which it is normal to get second and third chances? Do we feel the world is big enough, and reasonable enough, for us to have a legitimate shot at doing our own thing, or must we be subservient, meek serfs?

Testing Emotional Identity

It is symptomatic of the way our minds work that we cannot directly ask ourselves who we are in terms of Emotional Identity. We need to ask ourselves smaller questions and answer them without pausing too long, thereby attempting to bypass our rationalising filters. Then we need to wheel back and sift through our answers to assemble a plausible picture of who we might be emotionally.

We need to sit an Emotional Identity Questionnaire:

Emotional Identity
Questionnaire

Give a score to each of the statements below, on a scale from 1 to 5:

1 = That's not true.
2 = That's not very true, but there's a glimmer of recognition.
3 = I don't know – maybe, maybe not.
4 = A bit true, but I have a few reservations.
5 = Yes, that's true.

Self-Love

1. If people knew who I really was deep down, they would be shocked.
2. It can be embarrassing to ask where the bathroom is.
3. In relationships, it can feel pretty disturbing when someone you like starts to like you back.
4. I sometimes feel a bit disgusting.
5. When people approve of you, a lot of it comes down to what you've managed to achieve.

Candour

1. People tend to think too much.
2. I'm not a jealous person
3. I'm basically very sane.
4. I don't mind feedback in theory, but most of what I've received has been really off the mark.
5. There's far too much 'psychobabble' around these days.

Communication

1. People you're close to should be naturally good at understanding how you feel in a lot of areas.
2. When I feel misunderstood, I need to be alone.
3. I'm not a good teacher.
4. I sulk every now and then.
5. People rarely 'get it' when you're trying to explain.

Trust

1. It's not going to be OK in the end.
2. I worry about my health.
3. Civilisation is pretty fragile.
4. When someone is late, I sometimes wonder if they might have died.
5. If you don't watch them closely, people will try to swindle you.

Count up your scores in each category. The lower the score, the more you have of each quality. The higher the score, the less you have of Self-Love, Candour, Communicative skill and Trust.

Emotional
Inheritance

What creates Emotional Identity? Why do we have the Emotional Identity we do and not a different one?

A big modern response looks to genetics for answers: it tells us that we have a specific genetic inheritance and (via many complex processes) that this inheritance shapes our adult personality. We're not saying that genetics are irrelevant, but we want to focus attention on another kind of inheritance: Emotional Inheritance.

One of the characteristic possessions of all European nobles for many centuries was an elaborate depiction of their family tree, showing their lineage down the generations. The idea was that the person sitting at the bottom of the tree would see themselves as the product of – and the heir to – all who had come before them. The tree gave a quick visual guide to who they were and what others should know about them. If two aristocrats were contemplating marriage, the first thing they would do was to carefully examine each other's trees.

It can seem like a quaint preoccupation, wholly tied to

another age and solely of interest to members of a few grand and ancient families. But the idea of such a tree sits upon a universal and still highly relevant concern: irrespective of the financial and status details of our families, we all have another significant legacy to grapple with, in that each of us is the recipient of an emotional inheritance, largely unknown to us, yet enormously influential in determining our day-to-day behaviour, and normally in rather negative or complex directions. We need to understand the details of our Emotional Inheritance a little before we are able to ruin our own and others' lives by acting upon its often antiquated and troublesome dynamics.

Some of what we inherit psychologically from our families can, of course, be positive. Marcus Aurelius (121–180 CE), the philosopher and emperor of Rome, began his *Meditations* with a touching list of the many positive things he had learned from his relatives:

> From my grandfather Verus I learned good morals and the government of my temper.
> From my father, modesty and a manly character.
> From my mother, piety and beneficence, and abstinence, not only from evil deeds, but even from evil thoughts; and

further, simplicity in my way of living, far removed from
the habits of the rich.

– Marcus Aurelius, The Meditations (161-180 CE)

Few of us are as lucky as this. Alongside positives, we tend to inherit many predispositions that make it harder than necessary for us to cope with adult life, especially in the area of relationships and of work. Were we to repeat Marcus Aurelius's exercise, it might run in a far darker direction:

> *From my mother, I learnt to lose my temper quickly and*
> *give up on being heard properly by people close to me.*
> *From my father, I learnt to judge myself by my external*
> *achievements only and therefore to feel intense jealousy*
> *and panic in the face of professional setbacks.*

A lot in our inheritance works against our chances of fulfilment and well-being because its logic does not derive from the present; it involves a repetition of behaviour and expectations that were formed and learnt in childhood, typically as the best defence we could cobble together in our immaturity in the face of a situation bigger and more complex than we were.

Unfortunately, it is as if part of our minds hasn't realised the change in our external circumstances, but insists on re-enacting the original defensive manoeuvre even in front of people or at moments that don't warrant or reward it. For example, it might once have made sense to try to see the good side and attract the loyalty of a parent even though they were neglectful and sometimes violent: there were few other options when one was three. But to continue to associate affection with violence and neglect is to impose intolerably narrow restrictions on one's adult love choices.

Our Emotional Inheritance clings to us because it was bequeathed in conditions of total helplessness. The early years were periods of acute vulnerability. We were utterly at the mercy of the prevailing environment. We could not properly move, speak, control or contain ourselves; we could not calm ourselves down or recover our equilibrium. We had no choice about who to direct our feelings towards and no way to defend ourselves adequately against what injured us. We could not even string thoughts together, needing the language eventually lent to us by others in order to begin to interpret our requirements. Even in the most benign of circumstances, with only the best intentions at play, the possibilities for warps and distortions are enormous. Few of us ever come through entirely unscathed.

Psychotherapists have developed a special term to capture what we inherit emotionally from the past: they call it our 'transference'. In their view, each of us is constantly at risk of 'transferring' patterns of behaviour and feeling from the past to a present that doesn't realistically call for it. We feel a need to punish people who aren't to blame; we worry about a humiliation that isn't on the cards; we are compelled to betray as we were once betrayed, three decades before.

Ideally, we would build up a storehouse of knowledge of what exactly we had inherited (and from whom); a kind of emotional family tree that would show us, and others, the issues that had been transferred across generations and were liable to disrupt our lives today.

Learning to Deal
with Emotional
Inheritance

Maturity involves accepting with good grace that we are involved in multiple transferences, along with a commitment to try to disentangle them rationally. The job of growing up means realising with due humility the exaggerated dynamics we may constantly bring to situations and to monitor ourselves more accurately and more critically so as to improve our capacity to judge and act in the here and now with greater fairness and neutrality. The idea is to grow a little wiser as to where our troubles come from and around what areas of our lives we need to be especially careful.

Traditionally, family trees didn't just exist to tell people about themselves; they were public objects intended to convey to strangers what they needed to know about us. Before grand people got married, they would carefully scan each other's trees to know what was at stake. An emotional family tree would have a similar value in letting others know more about us in contexts when they might still be sympathetic, before we've had a chance to damage or enrage them with our inheritance. Knowing the risks of transference prioritises sympathy and understanding over irritation and judgement. We can come to see that sudden bursts of anxiety or hostility in others may not always be directly caused by us, and so should not always be met with fury or wounded pride. Bristling and condemnation can give way to compassion for the difficulties all of us have with our pasts.

In a perfect world, two people on an early dinner date would swap beautifully drawn family trees called, perhaps, 'My Emotional Inheritance'. Such a tree would also be something to give at a wedding and would be required at work, as a supplement to a CV. Having a complex Emotional Inheritance would not be a source of shame; the pride would be that one understood its constituent parts. We don't need people to be perfect; we simply need them to be able to explain the greater part of their inherited imperfections calmly and in good time, before we are enmeshed in the sufferings they can otherwise cause us.

Fully getting to grips with our Emotional Inheritance is a long-term task. It takes a lot of time and involves asking ourselves questions again and again. So, it is worth wondering what the point is of realising the ways our

Emotional Inheritance has shaped our current identity. There seem to be three major benefits of this therapeutic exercise:

1. We become aware of ways in which we are a bit crazy (that is: puzzling to others and inappropriate in our responses). We can catch ourselves before we do too much damage. But we also grasp why we are like this. We don't have to hate ourselves; we can become more sympathetic to our awkward legacies and realise that we have learnt a few somewhat counterproductive ways of coping.

2. We can more calmly explain ourselves to others. Even if we can't entirely change, we can flag up what might be challenging about living around us. If we understand ourselves better we can help others understand us more sympathetically too.

3. We begin to see that we have a degree of freedom and opportunity to change (to a limited but useful degree) the difficult parts of who we are. We don't have to keep on repeating exactly what we've been doing. There are other options.

Emotional
Inheritance
Questionnaire

Our Emotional Identities have a history; they are an Emotional Inheritance from our families. Knowing more about our Emotional Inheritance enables us to watch out for peculiar behaviour, feel sympathy for ourselves, explain ourselves to others and, in small ways, change.

Consider the inherited, familial aspects of the central pillars of your Emotional Identity:

Self-Love
- Did you feel loved?
- How much of who you really are were you allowed to be?
- Were you allowed to fail?
- Were you made to feel guilty and ashamed? How?
- How was the 'bad' side of you received?

Candour
- Did you have to be very normal?
- Did people around you admit to being afraid and sad?
- Did it matter what people thought?

Communication
- Did people communicate patiently and clearly
  with you?
- Were you allowed to tell others how you really felt?

Trust
- Were the people around you confident about the
  world?
- Did they panic acutely?
- Did they lose their temper regularly?
- How worried were they about your health?

Probe gently. Be sympathetic. If you get stuck, be patient.
Each answer might be a novel, or at least a short story.

IV
Honesty and Denial

A major obstacle to self-knowledge, and in turn, to a flourishing life, is the tendency of one part of the mind to lie to the other. We lie to ourselves for what might seem like a very understandable reason: we want to avoid pain. We become experts at pushing disturbing thoughts far into the unconscious because we are squeamish.

The things we lie to ourselves about

There are four things we particularly tend to lie to ourselves about:

1. Things we need to change about our lives
We lie about all the problematic aspects it would take considerable effort to alter: our jobs, our relationships, our friendships, our relations with our families, our health, our habits and our ideas.

2. Things that might disturb our self-image
We lie because we need to think well of ourselves and are devoted to imagining that we are essentially normal, without peculiar loves, hates and deviant thoughts.

3. Things we really want and can't have
We lie because we don't want to feel so inadequate, and yet because we lack so many good things.

4. Things we are angry with others about
We lie because we are furious with certain people who we are supposed to love. And we lie because what we are furious about feels so minor and petty for a grown-up to care about.

How we lie to ourselves

Given how risky the truth about us can feel, we have had to learn to be masters of deception. Our techniques are wide-ranging, devilish and often hugely imaginative. Here are some of the leading manoeuvres we employ to pull the wool over our own eyes:

Distraction or addiction

We identify something that can very effectively keep our thoughts away from troubling inner confrontations. Online pornography is a favourite, the news another, alcohol a third, work a fourth. We don't so much like these elements in and of themselves; we like them for their ability to keep us away from what we fear.

Manic cheeriness

A sadness that we haven't been able to admit to is often covered up with exaggerated doses of manic cheeriness. We aren't happy so much as incapable of allowing ourselves to feel even the slightest sadness, in case we were to be overwhelmed by our buried grief. We develop a brittle, insistent tendency to say that all is very well. 'This is lovely, isn't it?' we might press, leaving no room for any ideas to the contrary.

Irritability

Denied anger with a particular person or situation often seeps out into a generalised irritability. So successful is the lie, we don't really know what's up: we just keep losing our tempers. Someone has moved the TV remote, there aren't any eggs in the fridge, the electricity bill is slightly higher than expected... anything can set us off. Our brains are so filled with how frustrating and annoying things are that we have cleverly left no space for focusing on the true, very sad issue.

Denigration

We tell ourselves that we simply don't care about something – love or politics, career success or intellectual life, that beautiful student or the house we can't afford. And we are very emphatic about our lack of interest and disdain. We go to great lengths to make it clear to others and ourselves how absolutely unconcerned we are. There must be no mistake. We simply and absolutely don't care. They're all stupid. It's a waste of money. What idiots. We might go in for long, erudite and argumentative explanations about why something doesn't impress us. We get very rational and factual. We're being more eloquent and clever in fending off any idea that we might be interested in something than in defending anything we actually love.

Censoriousness

We grow censorious and deeply disapproving of certain kinds of behaviour and people. What we don't admit is that we are so full of condemnation only because we need to ward off awareness that a part of us in fact really likes the condemned element. We attack certain sexual tastes as deviant and beyond the pale, precisely because we half-know that we share them somewhere inside ourselves. We are delighted when particular people are arrested or shamed in the press; what they did was utterly awful, we insist, our outrage shielding us from any risk of spotting the connection between them and us.

When our feelings become very tricky, we just pass them on to someone else. Rather than accepting them as our own, we convince ourselves that they exist only in other people, who we duly attack and censor. Perhaps your partner has started speaking about a party being thrown by a moderately famous person. You're thrilled about it, but frightened to be thrilled. You are meant to be egalitarian and serious, so you can't want this. So, conveniently, it seems it must be just your partner who wants this, and you then accuse them of being a 'serious social climber'. You have found the perfect person on whom to land your unacceptable desires.

Defensiveness

When there is unwelcome news, we may resort to a highly successful diversionary tactic: taking offence. A colleague tries to give us a bit of feedback. Instantly we accuse them of rudeness, arrogance and a sense of entitlement. A partner points something out and we become furious that they are piling pressures on us at a difficult point. Feeling offended takes up all our attention. It muddies the waters. We no longer have to pay attention to information that is correct but challenging.

Cynicism or despair

We are sad about particular things, but confronting them would be so arduous that we generalise and universalise the sadness. We don't say that X or Y has made us sad; we say that everything is terrible and everyone is awful. We spread the pain in order that its particular, specific causes can no longer be the focus of attention. To put it metaphorically, our sadness becomes lost in the crowd.

The idea of being dishonest with ourselves may not sound especially decent, but why shouldn't we just lie if it is more pleasant to do so? What is the issue with keeping things from ourselves if we suffer so much from the truth? Why is the truth necessarily good?

The drawbacks of
lying to ourselves

The defence of honesty must ultimately be a cautionary, egoistic one. We need to tell ourselves the truth when we can for the simple reason that we often pay a high price for the short-term calm of our lies.

We miss key opportunities for growth and learning

The things we are in denial about are painful, but they simultaneously contain material that is potentially vital to our overall growth and development.

If we could stop, for a time, looking at naked people, or drinking, or checking the news, and face up to what we need to do, we might – gradually – end up in a much better place.

If we could accept that we wanted certain things, even if we didn't end up with all of them, we could still secure some sort of substitute or a portion of them.

If we could face up to our stranger desires, we'd learn to navigate more freely in our minds and be alive to a wider range of our own thoughts, which could render us more creative and interesting.

We're not nice to be around

Our defences might be hidden from ourselves, but their consequences are often evident to others. They are the ones who suffer our irritability, gloom, manufactured cheerfulness or our defensive rationalisations. We act unfairly, so they back off and keep a distance. We grow isolated and friendless.

We develop harmful symptoms

The truth will out. And when we don't let it emerge, it has a tendency to reveal itself through involuntary (often physical) symptoms. We become insomniac or impotent, an eyelid starts twitching, we acquire a stutter, we scream in our sleep, we lose energy, we fall into depression....

The way to greater honesty follows some of the techniques evident from the rehabilitation of crimes. We must reduce the shame and danger of confession. And we must improve the chances of rehabilitation.

To bolster the courage to look more frankly into ourselves, we need a broader, more reassuring sense of what is normal. Of course, it is normal to be envious, crude, sexual, weak, in need, child-like, grandiose, terrified and furious. It is normal to be excited by people who are younger and older than us and to desire random adventures even within loving and committed unions. It is normal to be hurt by signs of rejection, and to be made insecure by any evidence of neglect by a partner. It is normal to be weird; sometimes we want to jump on the railway tracks or lick the toilet seat. It is normal to harbour hopes for ourselves professionally far beyond what we have been able to achieve. It is normal to envy other people, many times a day, to be upset by any kind of criticism of our work or performance, and to be so sad that we think a lot of suicide or flight.

We don't think in this free and honest way because we're scared that we could never come back from such confessions. But recognising a feeling doesn't mean you follow it to a conclusion. Admitting to a fantasy or desire doesn't have to mean acting it out – in fact, it is usually an alternative to doing so.

Understanding how self-deceit works can help us with

ourselves, but also with others. We start to see them as beset by the same problems as us. Quite often they say things that are not in line with their true feelings or desires – mean things when they are feeling vulnerable, perhaps, or arrogant things when they are feeling small – and we will identify that it is charitable to forgive them for not always managing to be reliable correspondents of their inner lives. It is not sinister to think this way of others; it is a kindly move that gives us the energy to lend a second, more compassionate, look at behaviour that might initially appear horrifying.

Exercise:
An Experiment
in Honesty

Consider our list of defensive, self-deceiving moves:

- Distraction or addiction
- Manic cheeriness
- Irritability
- Denigration
- Censoriousness
- Defensiveness
- Cynicism or despair

We all practise them all the time.

Can you remember specific incidents in your life when you employed them as strategies? What were you trying to hide from yourself?

It can help if this exercise happens in a group, because the enemy of such an effort is often the sense that we're all alone. The solution is always the normalisation of the disavowed parts of ourselves.

V
Self-Judgement

The Inner Voice

Somewhere in our minds, removed from the day to day, there sits a judge. They watch what we do, study how we perform, examine the effect we have on others, track our successes and failures, and then, eventually, they pass a verdict. So consequential is this judgement, it colours our entire sense of ourselves. It determines our levels of confidence and self-compassion; it lends us a sense of whether we are worthwhile beings or conversely, should not really exist. The judge is in charge of what we call our self-esteem.

The verdict of the judge is more or less loving, more or less enthusiastic, but not according to any objective rulebook or statute. Two individuals can end up with wildly different levels of self-esteem even though they may have done much the same things. Certain judges simply seem more predisposed than others to lend us an essentially buoyant, warm, appreciative and generous view of ourselves. Others encourage us to be hugely critical, often disappointed and sometimes close to disgust.

The origin of the voice of the inner judge is simple to trace: it is an internalisation of the voice of people who were once outside us. We have absorbed the tone of a kind and gentle caregiver, who liked to laugh indulgently at our foibles and had endearing names for us, or else the voice of a harassed or angry parent; the menacing threats of an elder sibling keen to put us down; the words of a schoolyard bully, or a teacher who seemed impossible to please. We take in these voices because at certain key moments in the past they sounded so compelling and irresistible. The authority figures repeated their messages over and over until they became lodged in our own way of thinking – for better and for worse.

Exercise:
An Audit of
Our Inner Voice

We can catch the sound of what our inner voice is like when we prompt ourselves to finish certain sentences:

- When I do something stupid, I usually tell myself...
- When I succeed, I usually tell myself...
- When I'm feeling lazy, my inner voice says...
- When I think of what I want sexually, my inner voice says...
- When I get angry with someone, my inner voice says...

Does the inner judge strike you as kindly or punitive?

Whose outer voice became your inner voice in the context of each question?

Why the Inner
Voice Matters

Our level of self-love is very consequential across our lives. It can be tempting to suppose that being hard on ourselves, although painful, is ultimately useful. Self-flagellation can feel like a survival strategy that steers us clear of the many dangers of indulgence and complacency. But there are equal, if not greater, dangers in an ongoing lack of sympathy for our own plight. Despair, depression and suicide are not minor risks.

Afflicted by a lack of self-love, romantic relationships become almost impossible, for one of the central requirements of a capacity to accept the love of another turns out to be a confident degree of affection for ourselves, built up over the years, largely in childhood. We need a legacy of feeling that we in some basic way deserve love in order not to respond obtusely to affections granted to us by prospective adult partners. Without a decent amount of self-love, the kindness of another will always strike us as misguided or fake, even as strangely insulting, for it suggests that they haven't even begun to understand us, so different are our relative assessments of what we happen to deserve. We end up self-destructively

– although unconsciously – disappointing the intolerable, unfamiliar love that has been offered to us by someone who clearly has no clue who we are.

Changing the
Inner Voice

It may feel tempting to say that we shouldn't judge ourselves at all. We should simply approve and love. But a good internal voice is rather like (and just as important as) a genuinely decent judge; someone who needs to separate good from bad but who can be merciful, fair, accurate in understanding what's going on and interested in helping us deal with our problems. It's not that we should stop judging ourselves; rather that we should learn to be better judges of ourselves.

Part of improving how we judge ourselves involves learning – in a conscious, deliberate way – to speak to ourselves in a new and different manner, and this means exposing ourselves to better voices. We need to hear constructive, kindly voices often enough and around tricky enough issues that they come to feel like normal and natural responses – so that, eventually, they become our own thoughts.

One approach is to identify a nice voice we knew in the past and give it more scope. Perhaps there was a kindly grandmother or aunt who was quick to see our side of things and who would offer us deft words of encouragement. When things don't go as we want, we can ask ourselves what this person would say – and then actively rehearse to ourselves the words of consolation they would most likely have offered (we'll tend to know immediately).

The other major strategy for changing the voices in our heads is to try to become an imaginary friend to ourselves. In friendship, we know instinctively how to deploy strategies of wisdom and consolation that we stubbornly refuse to apply to ourselves.

There are three key moves a good friend would typically make that can provide a model for what we should, with a new commitment to self-love, be doing with ourselves in our own heads. Firstly, a good friend likes you pretty much as you are already. Any suggestion they make, or ambition they have about how you could change, builds on a background of acceptance. When they propose that you might try a different tack, it's not an ultimatum or a threat. They are emphatically not saying that you have to change or be abandoned. The friend insists that we are good enough already. But they want to join forces with us to solve a challenge they feel we would properly benefit from overcoming.

Without being flattering, good friends also constantly keep in mind certain things we're getting right. They don't think anything wrong with the odd compliment and emphasis on our strengths. It's quite galling how easily we can lose sight of all of our good points when troubles strike. The friend doesn't fall into this trap; they can acknowledge the difficulties while still holding on to a memory of our virtues. The good friend is compassionate. When we fail, as we will, they are understanding and generous around our mishaps. Our folly doesn't exclude us from the circle of their love. The good friend deftly conveys that to err, fail and screw up is what we humans do. We all emerged from childhood with various biases in our character that evolved to help us cope with our necessarily imperfect parents. These acquired habits of mind will reliably let us down in adult life. But we're not to be blamed, because we didn't deliberately set out to be like this. We didn't realistically have a lot of better options. The good friend knows that failures are not, in fact, rare. They bring, as a starting point, their own and humanity's vivid experience of messing up into play as key points of reference. They are continually telling us that our specific case might be unique but that the general structure is common. People don't just sometimes fail. Everyone fails; we just don't know about it.

It is ironic, yet essentially hopeful, that we usually know quite well how to be a better friend to near strangers than we know how to be to ourselves. The hopefulness lies in the fact that we already possess the relevant skills of friendship. It's just that we haven't yet directed them to the person who probably needs them most – namely, of course, ourselves.

VI
Emotional
Scepticism

The outcome of any concerted attempt at self-knowledge could be presumed to be a deep understanding of ourselves. But strangely, the real outcome is rather different. It appears that the more closely we explore our minds, the more we start to see how many tricks these organs can play on us – and therefore the more we will appreciate how often we are likely to misjudge situations and our own emotions. A successful search for self-knowledge should end up with an admission of how little we do – and perhaps ever can – properly know of ourselves. It is an apparent paradox summed up by Socrates: *I am wise not because I know, but because I know I don't know.*

This critical attitude towards our own minds can be given a special name: Emotional Scepticism. Emotional Scepticism involves remaining highly cautious around our instincts, impulses, convictions and strong passions. Our brains are brilliant instruments, able to reason, synthesise, remember and imagine at an extraordinary pitch and rate. But these brains – let's call them walnuts in honour of their appearance – are also very subtly and dangerously flawed machines. They are flawed in ways that typically don't announce themselves to us and therefore give us few clues as to how on guard we should be about our mental processes. Most of the walnut's flaws can be attributed to the way the instrument evolved over millions of years. It emerged to deal with threats, some of which are no longer with us; at the same time, it had no chance to develop adequate responses to a myriad of challenges generated by our own complex societies.

A successful
search for self-
knowledge should
end up with an
admission of how
little we do – and
perhaps ever can
– properly know of
ourselves.

The flaws of the faulty walnut

We should feel pity for the walnut's situation and compassion for ourselves. But we should also remain very vigilant. Here are just some of the many things we need to watch out for with our faulty walnuts:

The walnut is influenced by the body to an extent it doesn't recognise

The walnut is extremely bad at understanding why it is having certain thoughts and ideas. It tends to attribute them to objective conditions out in the world, rather than seeing that they might be stemming from the impact of the body upon the mind. It doesn't typically notice the role that levels of sleep, sugar, hormones and other physiological factors play upon the formation of ideas. The walnut adheres to an intellectual interpretation of plans and positions that are, at base, frequently merely physiological. Therefore, it can feel certain that the right answer is to divorce or leave the job rather than go back to bed or eat something to raise blood sugar levels.

The walnut is influenced by its past, but can't see its distortions

The walnut believes it is judging each new situation on its own merits, but it is inevitably drawing upon patterns of action and feeling shaped in previous years. It might, for example, assume that any older man who speaks in a confident way is out to humiliate them, when actually it was just one man – their father – who did this.

The walnut is bad at self-control and gets passionate about, and scared of, the wrong things

The walnut constantly gets excited about things that aren't good for it: sugar, salt and sex with strangers, for a start. Advertising knows how to exploit this cognitive frailty to perfection. Our confusions can generally be traced back to targets that would once have been crucial and fitting for us to focus on in simpler environments, but cause chaos in the complicated conditions of modernity.

The walnut is egocentric

The walnut is primed to look at things from its own point of view – or the way of looking that is long established as normal in its tribe. It often simply can't believe that there are other ways of considering an issue. Other people can therefore seem perverse, or horrible to it – sparking outrage or self-pity. It's only in the last second, from an evolutionary point of view, that the walnut has started to try to imagine what it might be like to be someone else (a symptom of this is that it's learnt to take pleasure in novels). But this is still a fragile empathetic capacity, which tends to collapse, especially when the walnut is tired, and someone is trying to persuade it of a strange-sounding idea.

The Characteristics
of the Emotional
Sceptic

There are three key things that characterise the outlook of an emotionally sceptical person.

They distinguish between feeling and action

They don't automatically act on their feelings. The sceptic opens up the equivalent of a demilitarised zone between emotions and actions. Having surveyed the fragilities of our minds, the Ancient Greek Sceptics recommended that we learn to develop an attitude of what they called *epoché*, translated as 'reserve' or 'suspension of judgement'. Aware of our proclivities to error, we should never rush into decisions; we should let our ideas settle so they can be re-evaluated at different points in time. We are to be especially vigilant about the impact of sexual excitement, tiredness and public opinion on the formation of our plans.

They are modest about rationality

They are deeply conscious of the ways in which what seems

like pure cold reason is in fact the slave of passion. The emotional sceptic acknowledges that they can't be sure that what they feel is right actually is right. They become more modest, more ready to admit that there might be something to be said on the other's side, more open to ideas that strike them as initially implausible. Their scepticism leads them to be more generous to others and more modest in their own claims.

They are open to revising their beliefs and attitudes

They may feel pretty sure and committed just now but they are aware that their conclusions are provisional. The emotional sceptic knows there is more in their minds that they can access at any given point, and so remain tentative about their initial positions.

Our vulnerability to emotional distortion is not our fault: it is the result of a mismatch between the system of reasoning we have been bequeathed by our evolutionary history and the complex nature of the life tasks we are challenged by. We can't wholly refashion who we are: we will inevitably be swept about by egotism, jealousy, wounded pride, projection and bursts of tired panic and anger. In other words, we are condemned by nature to address the world and shape our lives via the mechanisms of an at times catastrophically faulty brain.

However, we will go a long way to counteract the problems of our machinery if we prepare ourselves for it; if we accept that we stare out at reality through a highly unreliable and distorted pane of glass and must, therefore, frequently suspend judgement, moderate our impulses, watch over our diet, and strive to get to bed early.

We will finally have learnt how to know ourselves when we have a complete picture at once of what we can know – and of what we have to remain very modest about ever knowing.

The School of Life is a global organisation helping people lead more fulfilled lives. It is a resource for helping us understand ourselves, for improving our relationships, our careers and our social lives – as well as for helping us find calm and get more out of our leisure hours. We do this through films, workshops, books, gifts and community. You can find us online, in stores and in welcoming spaces around the globe.